Maths Today
for ages 5-6

Numbers

Addition

Subtraction

Time

Money

Shape

Numbers

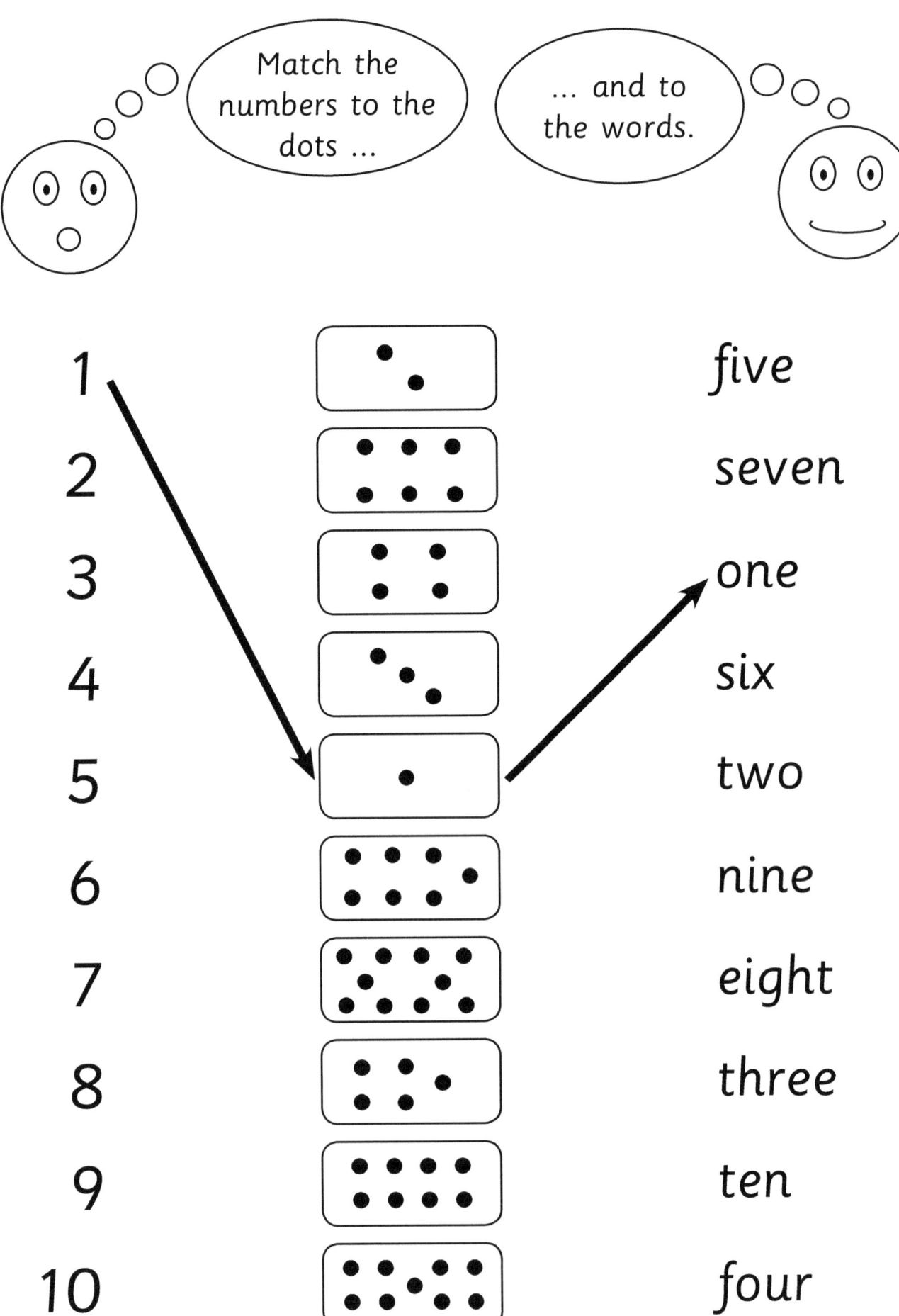

five

seven

one

six

two

nine

eight

three

ten

four

1

2

3

4

5

6

7

8

9

10

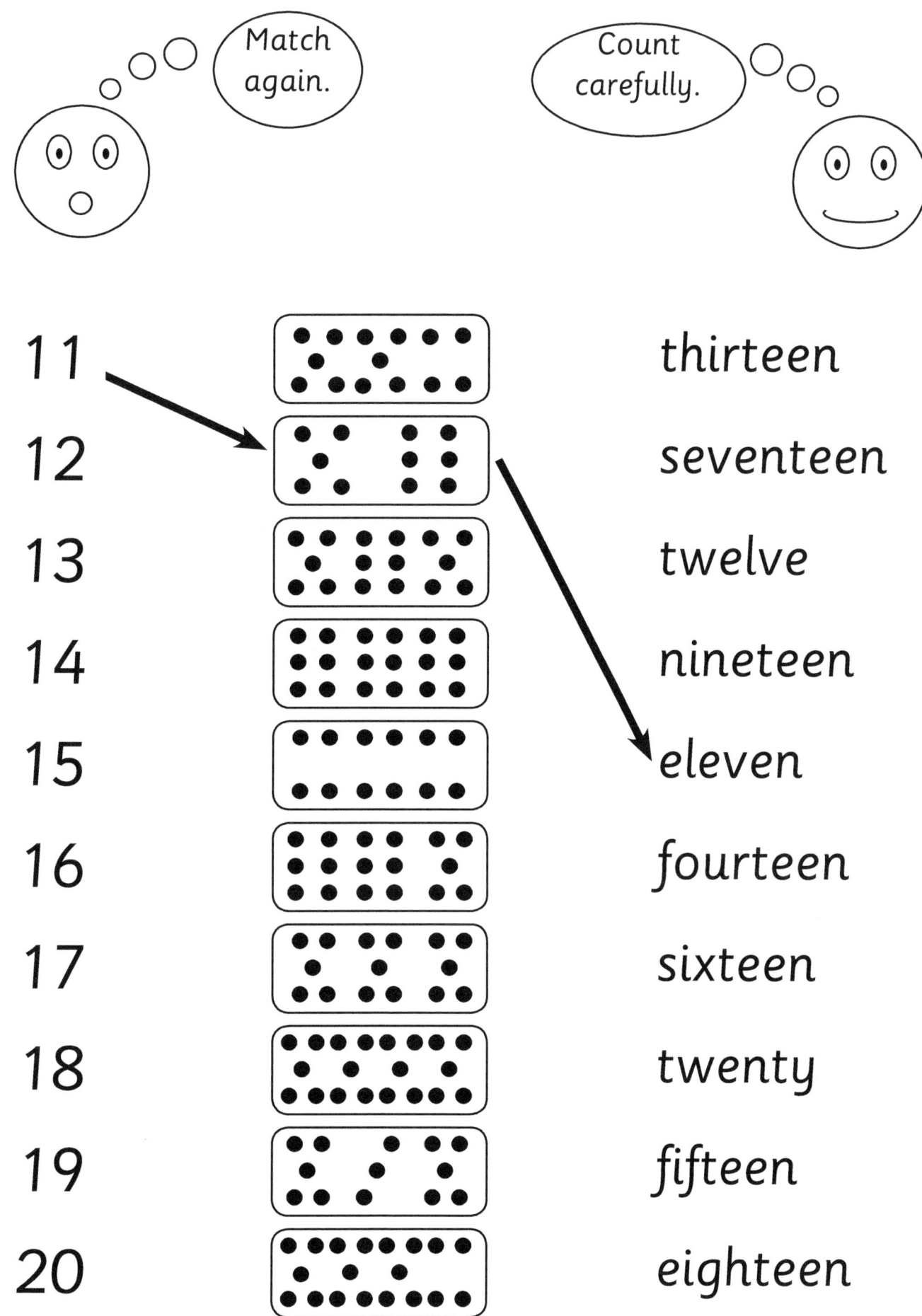

Writing numbers

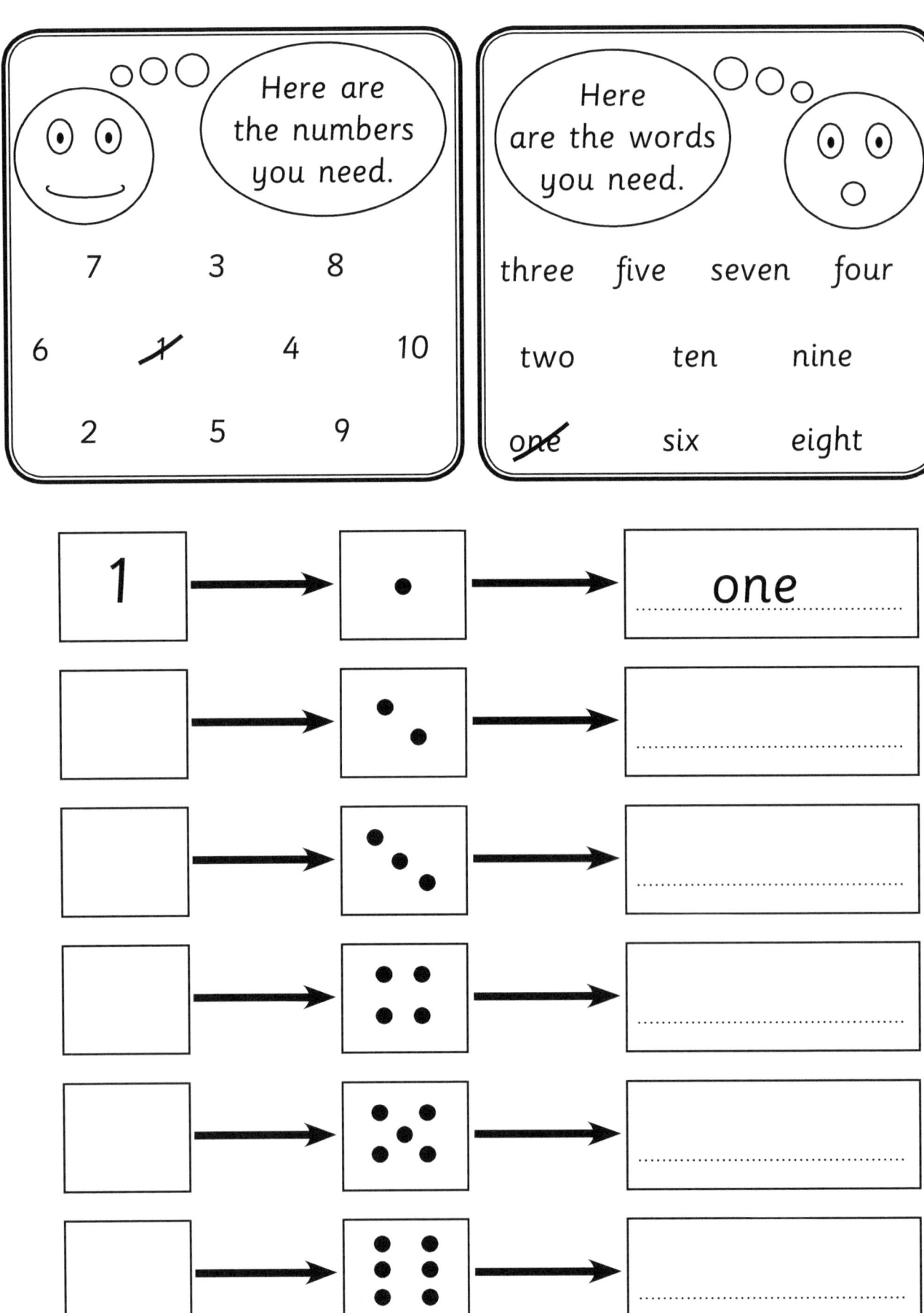

Here are the numbers you need.

7   3   8

6   1   4   10

2   5   9

Here are the words you need.

three   five   seven   four

two   ten   nine

one   six   eight

1	•	one
	••	
	•••	
	••••	
	•••••	
	••••••	

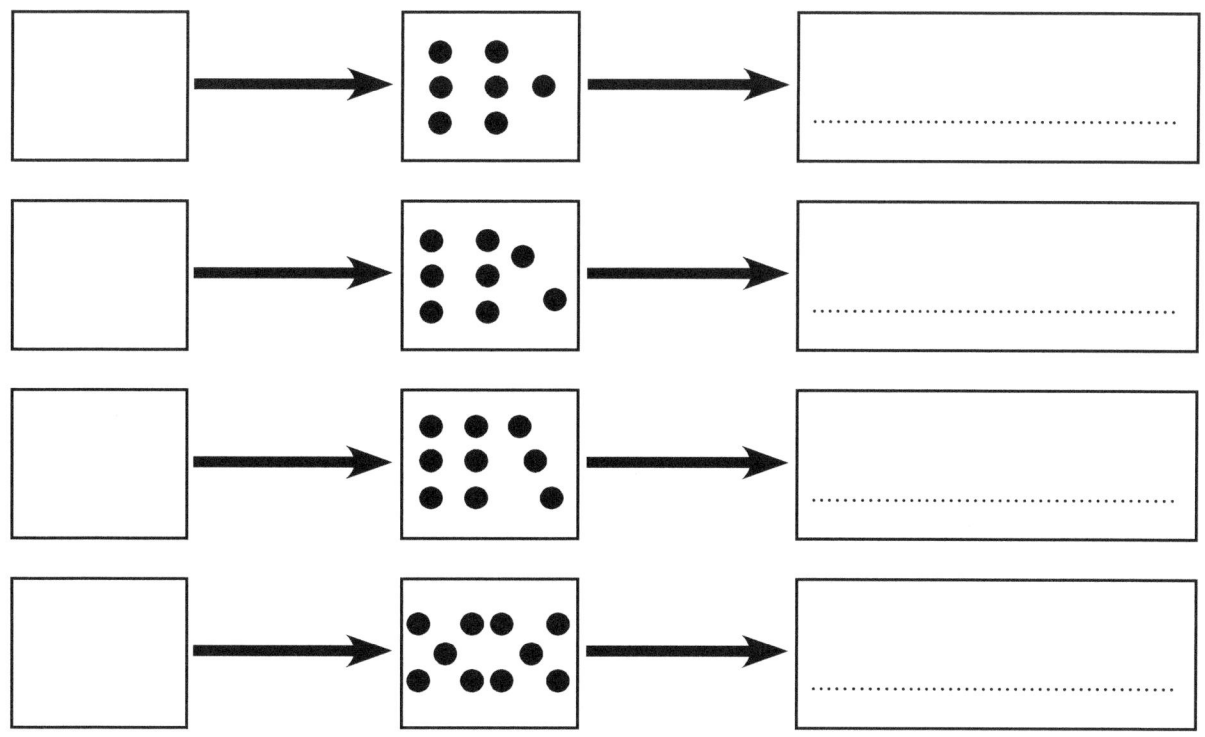

Join the dots.

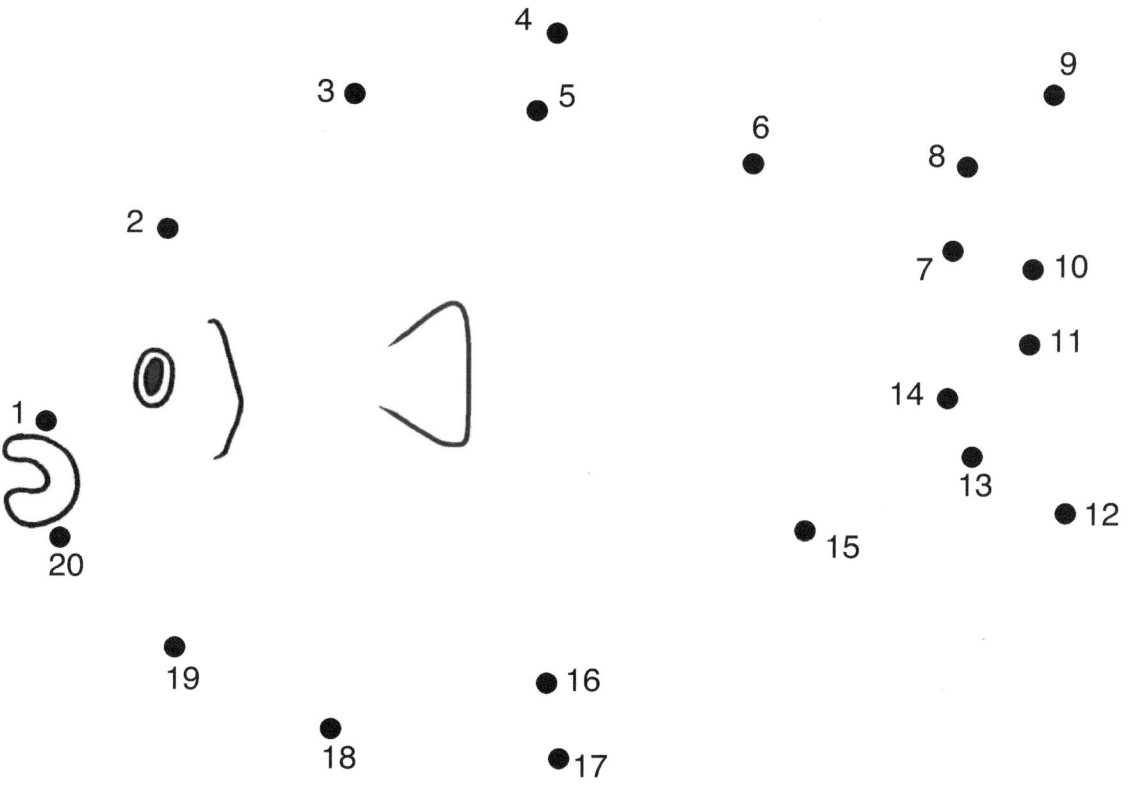

Writing more numbers

Numbers	Words
13　　12　　17 19　　11　　　14　　20 15　　16　　18	eleven　　　fourteen twelve　　　twenty eighteen　　sixteen fifteen　　seventeen thirteen　　nineteen

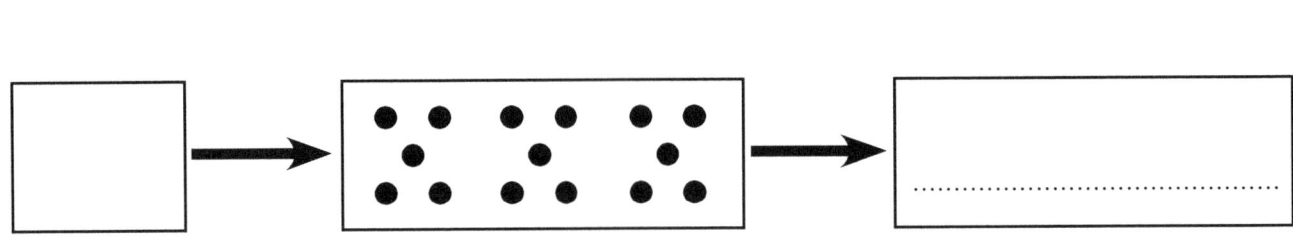

11 → eleven

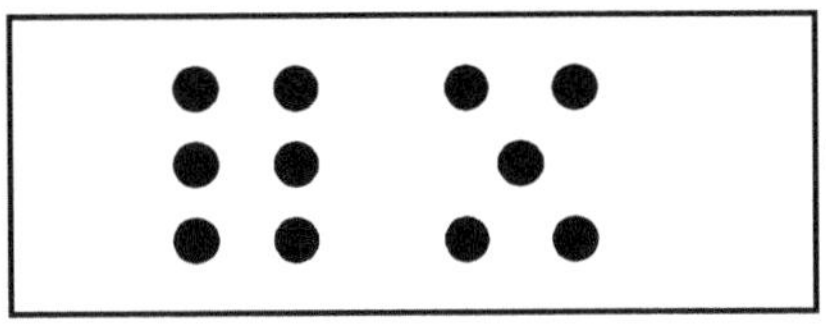

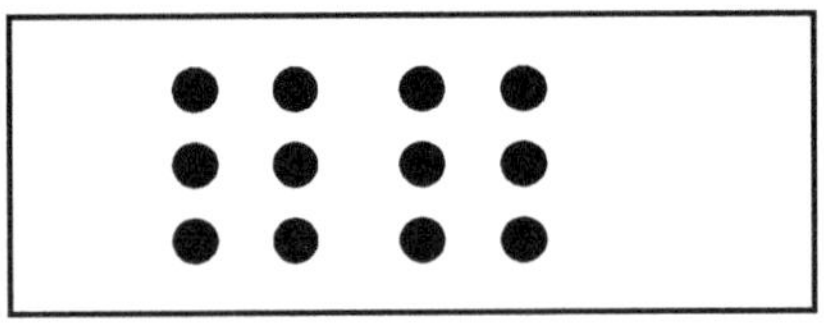

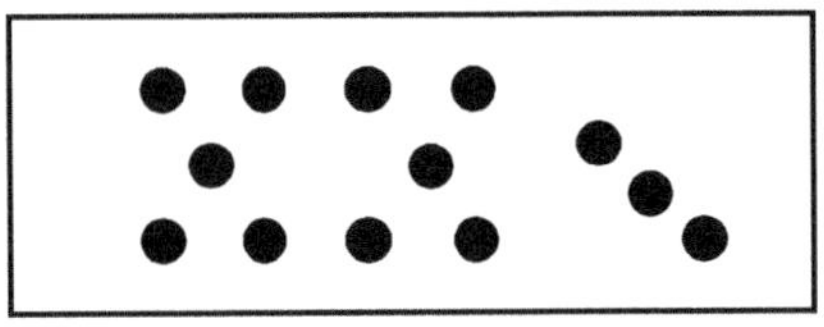

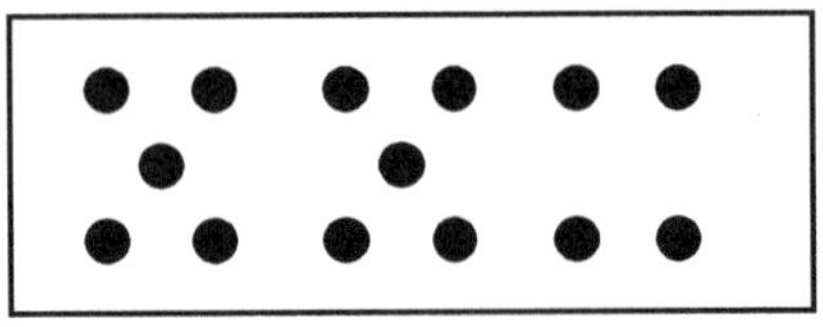

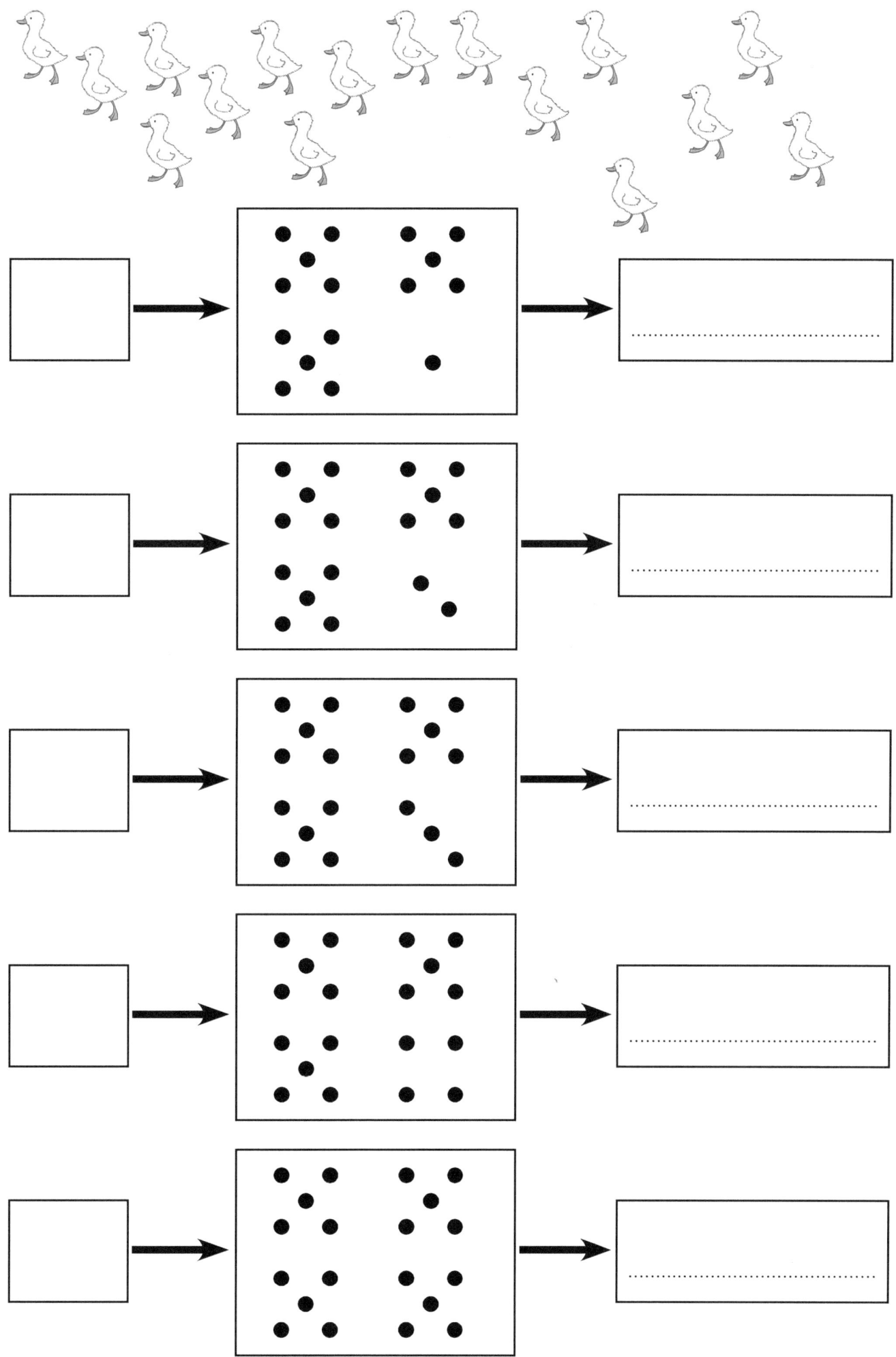

Missing numbers

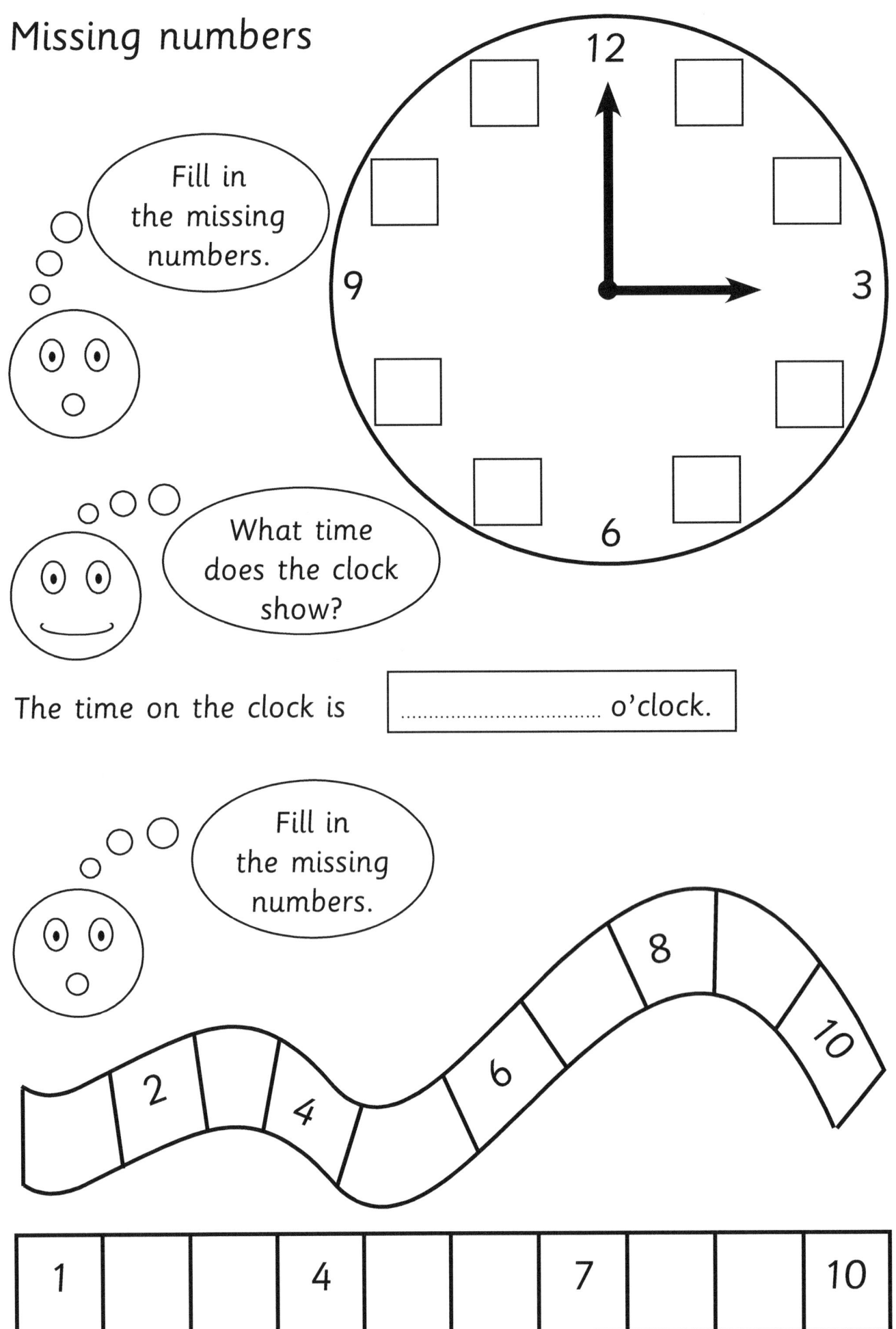

Fill in the missing numbers.

What time does the clock show?

The time on the clock is | .... o'clock. |

Fill in the missing numbers.

8

10

6

4

2

| 1 | | | 4 | | | 7 | | | 10 |

8

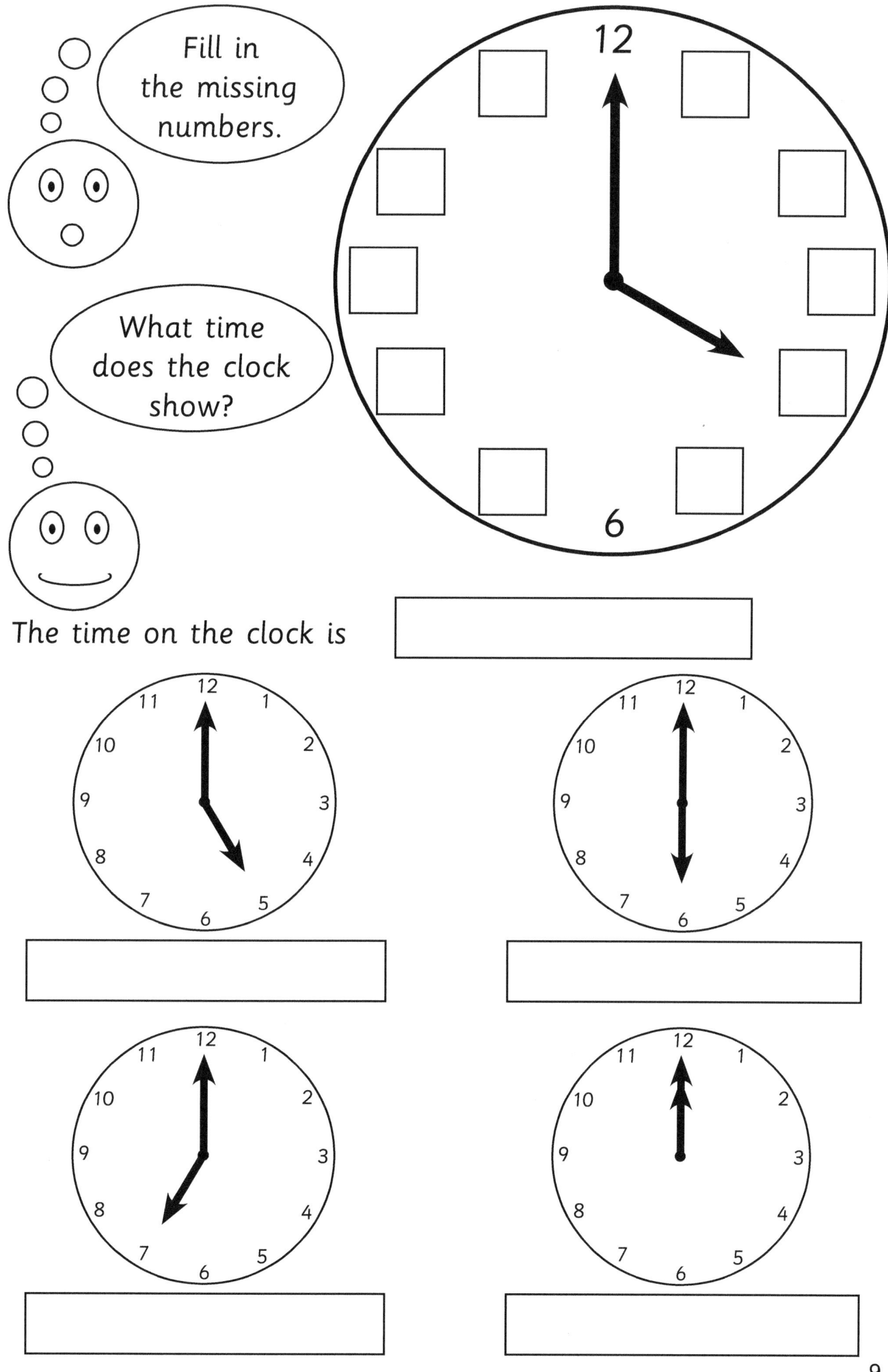

Fill in the missing numbers.

What time does the clock show?

The time on the clock is

9

Time and numbers

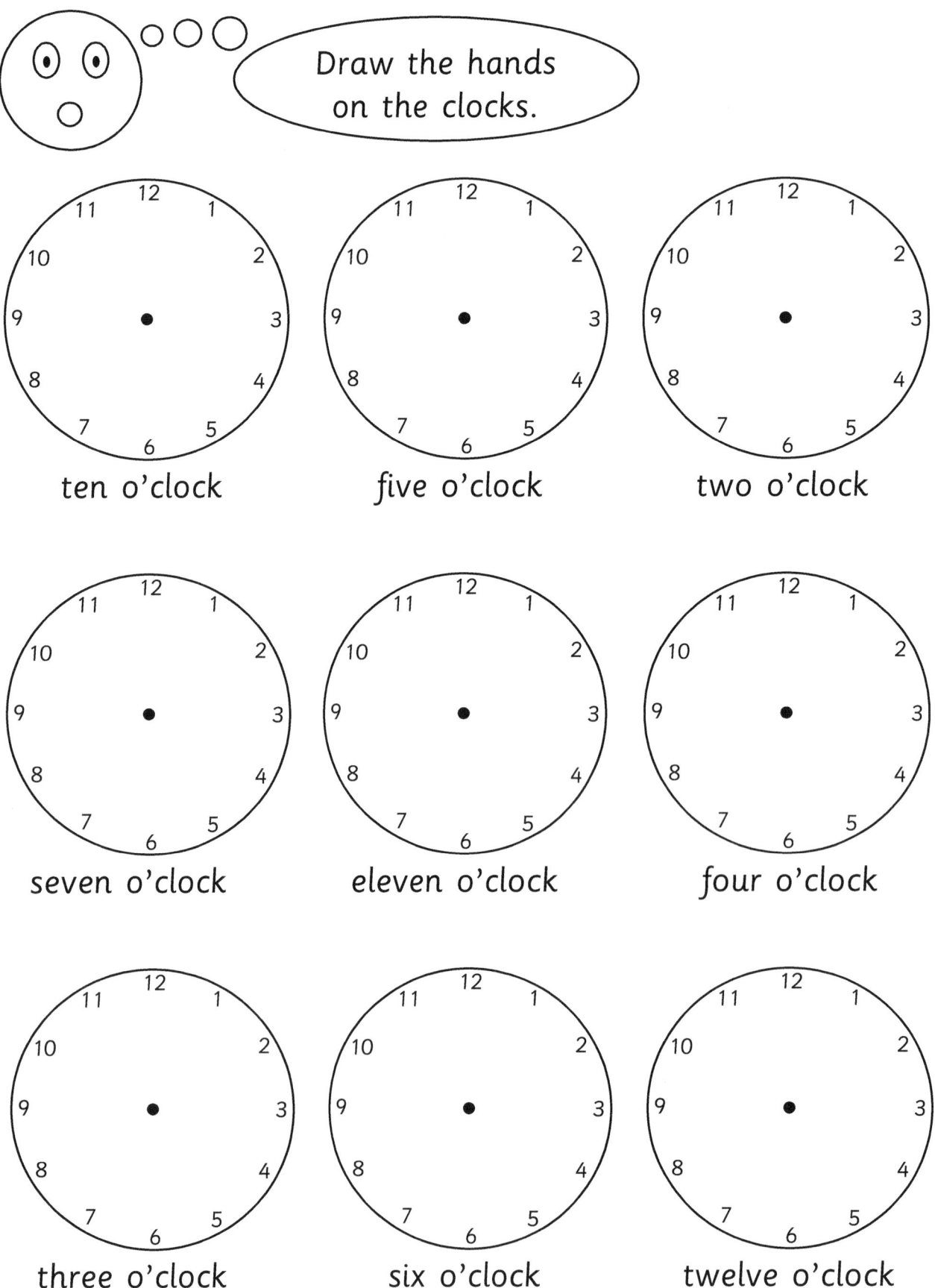

Draw the hands on the clocks.

ten o'clock

five o'clock

two o'clock

seven o'clock

eleven o'clock

four o'clock

three o'clock

six o'clock

twelve o'clock

Addition

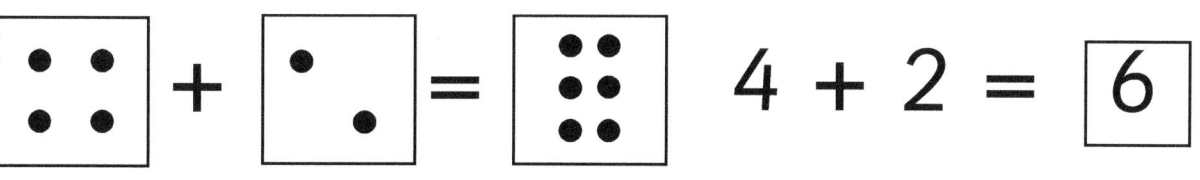

Draw
the dots

Write the
numbers

4 + 2 = 6

3 + 1 =

4 + 1 =

2 + 3 =

3 + 3 =

2 + 2 =

4 + 3 =

Number bonds

Look at how we can make 3.

Making 3

● ● ●

0 + 3 = 3

1 + 2 = 3

2 + 1 = 3

3 + 0 = 3

Fill in the gaps for the other numbers.

Making 4

0 + 4 = 4

1 + 3 = 4

2 + ☐ = 4

3 + ☐ = 4

4 + ☐ = 4

Making 5

0 + 5 = 5

1 + 4 = 5

2 + ☐ = 5

3 + ☐ = 5

4 + ☐ = 5

5 + ☐ = 5

Making 6

● ● ● ● ● ●

6 = ☐ + 6

6 = ☐ + 5

6 = ☐ + 4

6 = ☐ + 3

6 = ☐ + 2

6 = ☐ + 1

6 = ☐ + 0

Making 7

● ● ● ● ● ● ●

7 = ☐ + 7

7 = ☐ + 6

7 = ☐ + 5

7 = ☐ + 4

7 = ☐ + 3

7 = ☐ + 2

7 = ☐ + 1

7 = ☐ + 0

Find some ways to make 8.

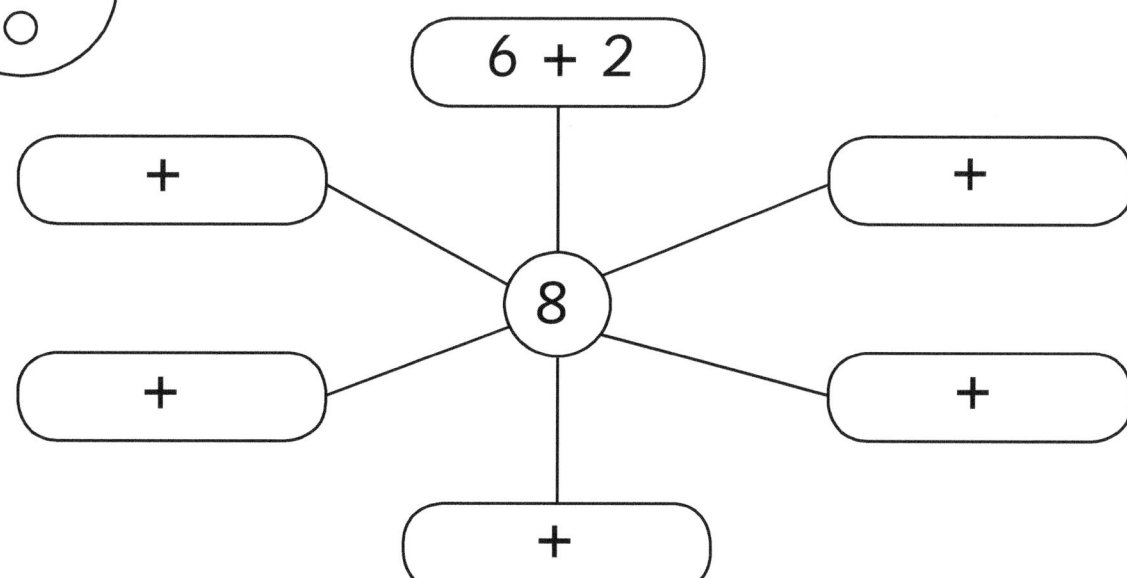

6 + 2

☐ +

☐ +

8

☐ +

☐ +

☐ +

More addition

Use your fingers if you want to.

4 + 2 = ☐

5 + 1 = ☐

3 + 3 = ☐

3 + 1 = ☐

2 + 2 = ☐

4 + 3 = ☐

5 + 2 = ☐

6 + 1 = ☐

3 + 2 = ☐

4 + 1 = ☐

Add by jumping 2.

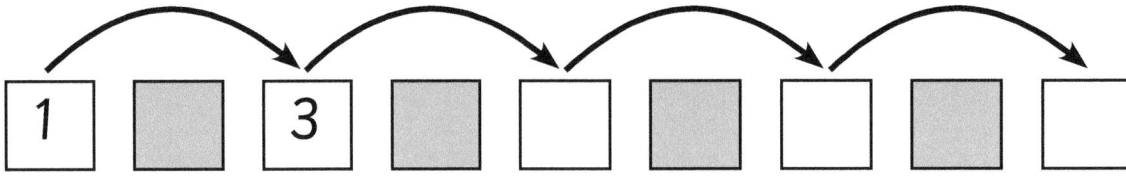

| 1 | | 3 | | | | | | |

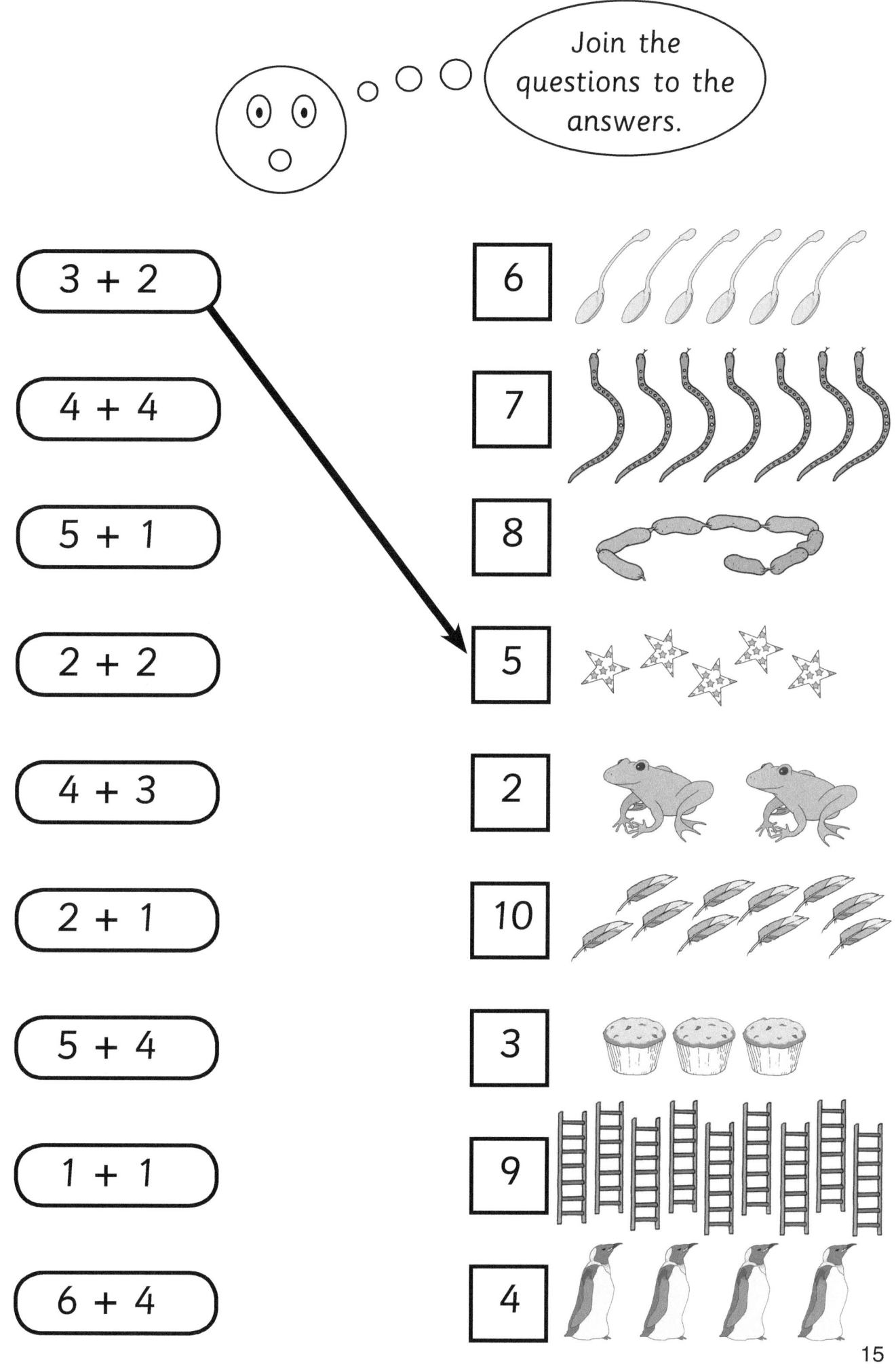

3 + 2

4 + 4

5 + 1

2 + 2

4 + 3

2 + 1

5 + 4

1 + 1

6 + 4

6

7

8

5

2

10

3

9

4

Triangles and squares

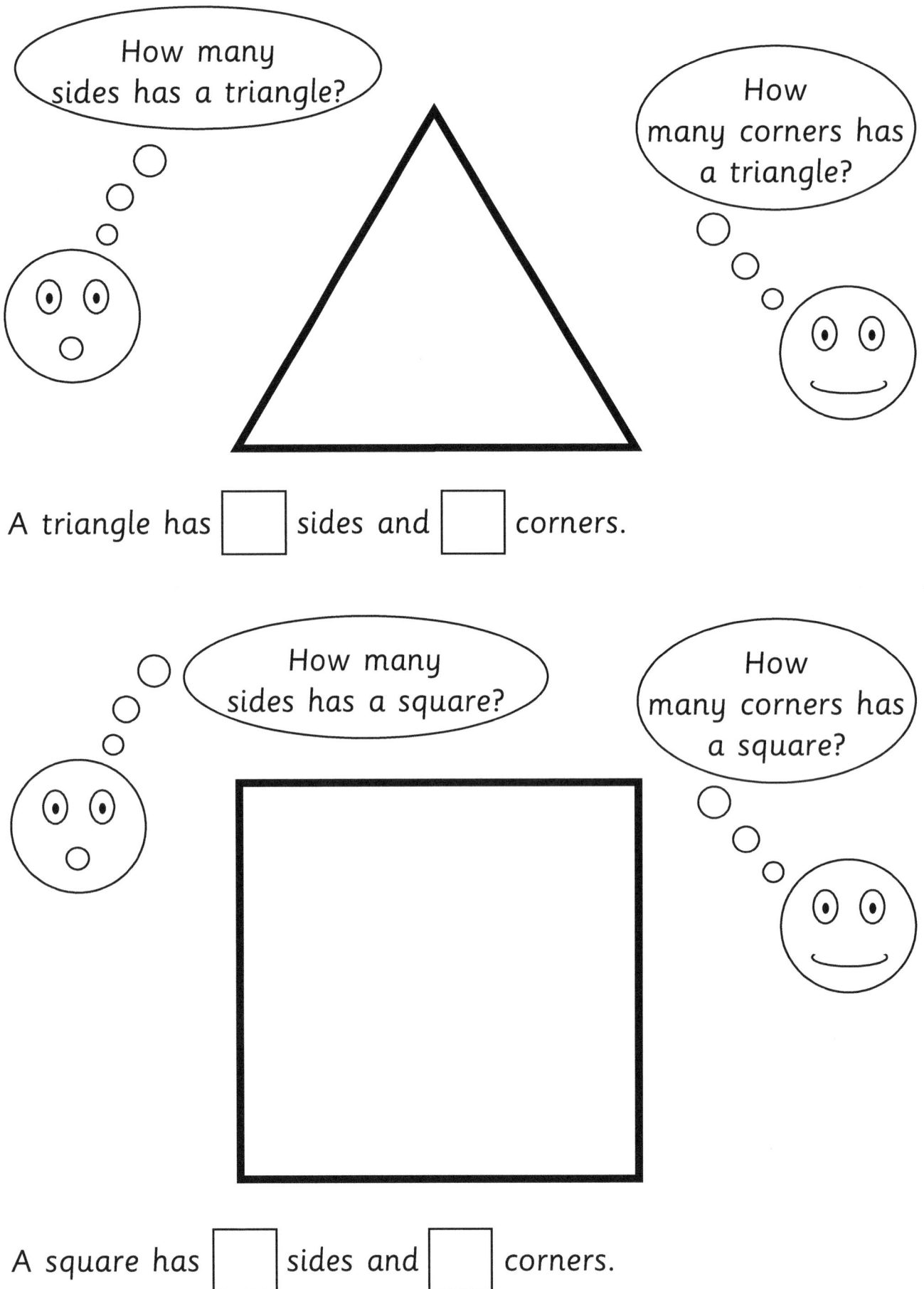

How many sides has a triangle?

How many corners has a triangle?

A triangle has ☐ sides and ☐ corners.

How many sides has a square?

How many corners has a square?

A square has ☐ sides and ☐ corners.

Join the dots to draw some triangles.

○ 1   ○ 2

○ 3

● 1

● 2

● 3

Join the dots to draw some squares.

○ 1   ○ 2

○ 4   ○ 3

● 1   ● 2

● 4   ● 3

Subtraction

If you have
four sweets, then
you eat one ...

... you will
only have three
sweets left.

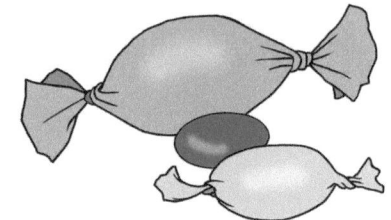

$$4 - 1 = 3$$

● ● ● ● ●
$5 - 1 = \boxed{}$

● ● ● ● ●
$5 - 2 = \boxed{}$

● ● ● ●
$4 - 1 = \boxed{}$

● ● ● ●
$4 - 2 = \boxed{}$

● ● ● ● ● ●
$6 - 1 = \boxed{}$

● ● ● ● ● ●
$6 - 2 = \boxed{}$

Subtracting from 6

6 − 1 = ☐

6 − 2 = ☐

6 − 3 = ☐

6 − 4 = ☐

6 − 5 = ☐

6 − 6 = ☐

Subtracting from 5

5 − 1 = ☐

5 − 2 = ☐

5 − 3 = ☐

5 − 4 = ☐

5 − 5 = ☐

Subtracting from 4

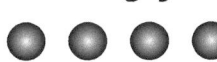

4 − 1 = ☐

4 − 2 = ☐

4 − 3 = ☐

4 − 4 = ☐

Subtracting from 3

3 − 1 = ☐

3 − 2 = ☐

3 − 3 = ☐

Subtracting from 2

2 − 1 = ☐

2 − 2 = ☐

Subtracting from 1

1 − 1 = ☐

Days of the week

Monday is the **first** school day of the week.

Tuesday is the **second** school day of the week.

Wednesday is the **third** school day of the week.

Thursday is the **fourth** school day of the week.

Friday is the **fifth** school day of the week.

Saturday is the first day of the weekend.

Sunday is the second day of the weekend.

Write the days of the week.

We have written the first one for you.

Monday

There are 7 days in a week.

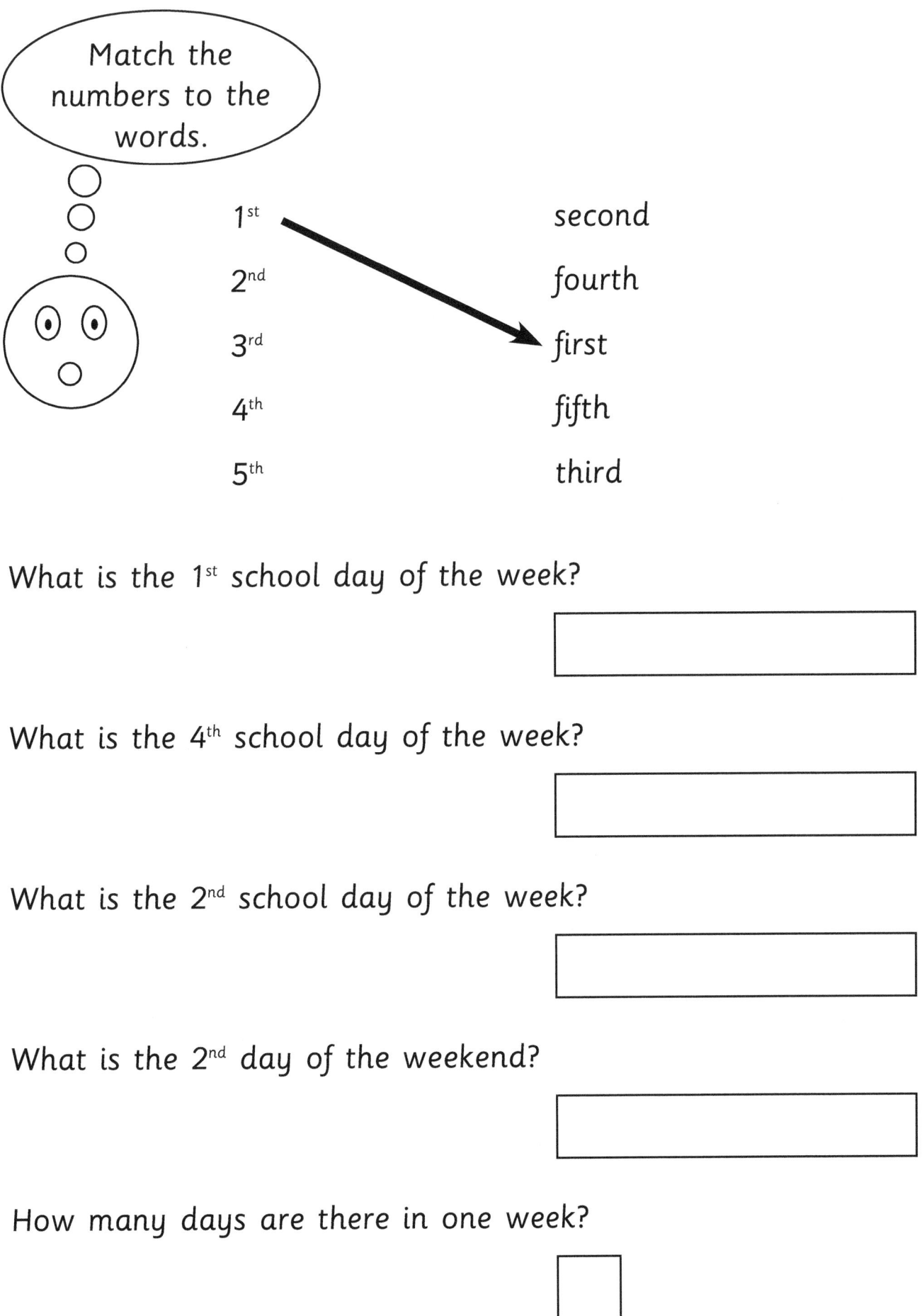

Match the numbers to the words.

1st	second
2nd	fourth
3rd	first
4th	fifth
5th	third

What is the 1st school day of the week?

What is the 4th school day of the week?

What is the 2nd school day of the week?

What is the 2nd day of the weekend?

How many days are there in one week?

Addition and Subtraction

You can use your fingers if you want to.

Look: $2 + 1 = 3$

$3 - 1 = 2$

$3 - 2 = 1$

$4 + 2 =$ 6

$6 - 4 =$ ☐

$6 - 2 =$ ☐

$3 + 2 =$ 5

$5 - 3 =$ ☐

$5 - 2 =$ ☐

$4 + 3 =$ 7

$7 - 3 =$ ☐

$7 - 4 =$ ☐

$5 + 4 =$ ☐

$9 - 4 =$ ☐

$9 - 5 =$ ☐

$5 + 3 =$ 8

$8 - 3 =$ ☐

$8 - 5 =$ ☐

$4 + 6 =$ 10

$10 - 4 =$ ☐

$10 - 6 =$ ☐

Doubles

1 + 1 = ☐

2 + 2 = ☐

3 + 3 = ☐

4 + 4 = ☐

5 + 5 = ☐

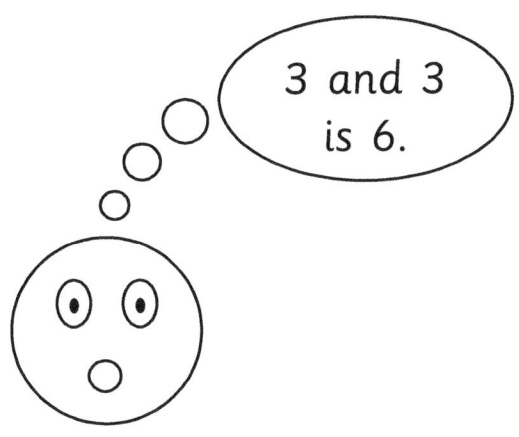

3 and 3 is 6.

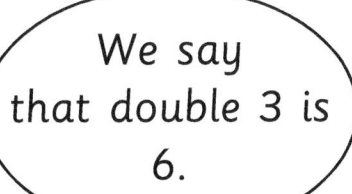

We say that double 3 is 6.

2 + 2 = ☐

5 + 5 = ☐

6 + 6 = ☐

Double 2 = ☐

Double 5 = ☐

Double 6 = ☐

Halves

3 + 3 = 6   so half of 6 = 3

half of 4 = ☐

half of 8 = ☐

half of 10 = ☐

half of 2 = ☐

half of 12 = ☐

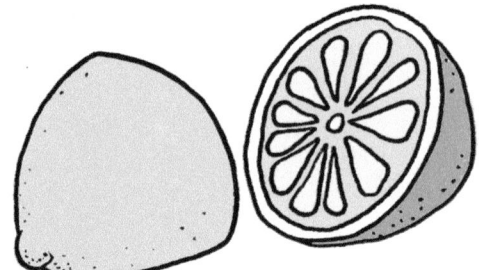

Colour half of these beads red.

Colour half of this
circle blue.

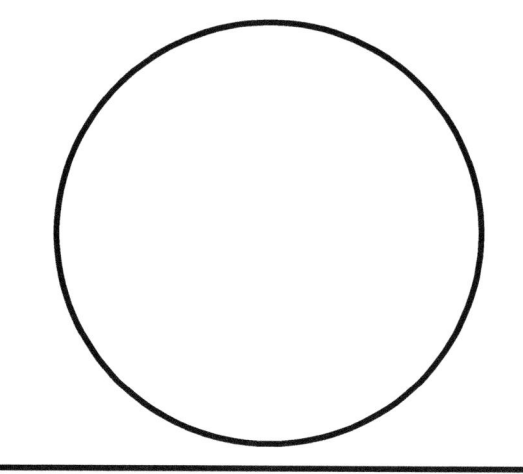

Colour half of this
square green.

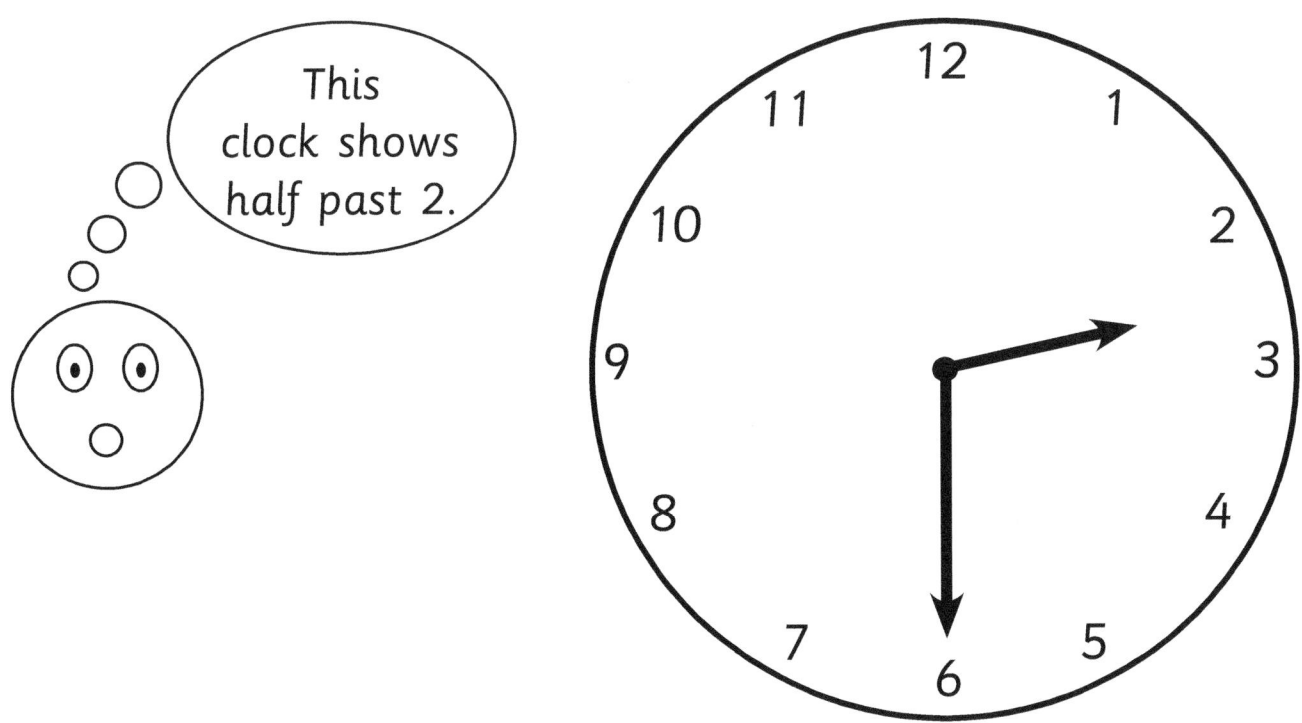

This clock shows half past 2.

12
1
2
3
4
5
6
7
8
9
10
11

What times do these clocks show?

....

....

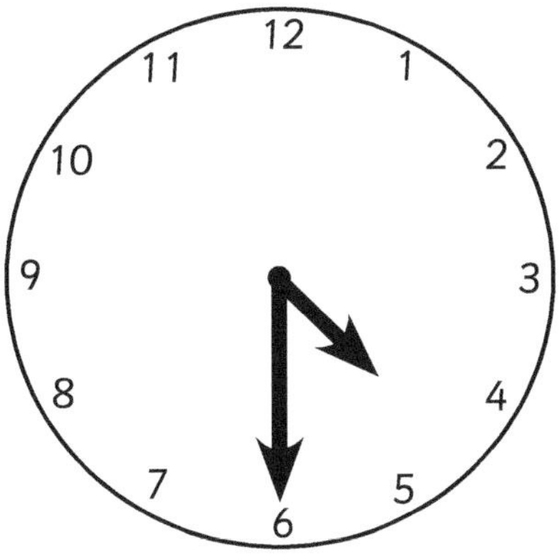

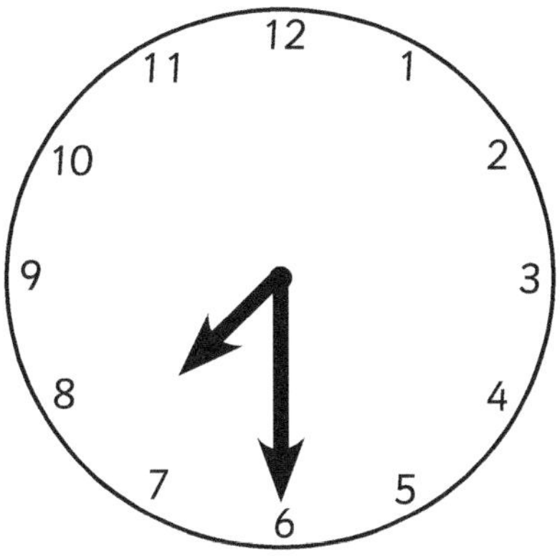

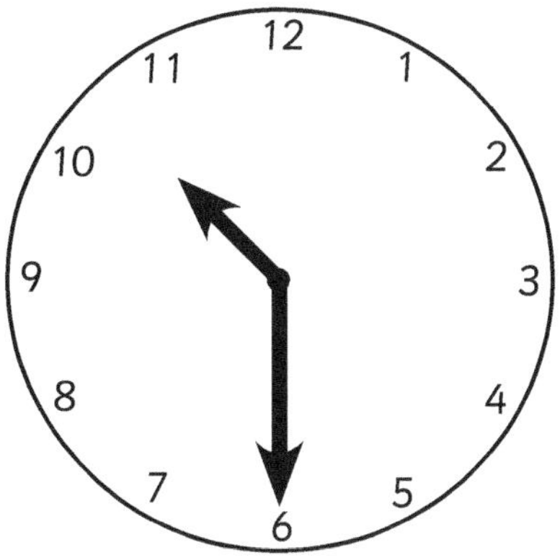

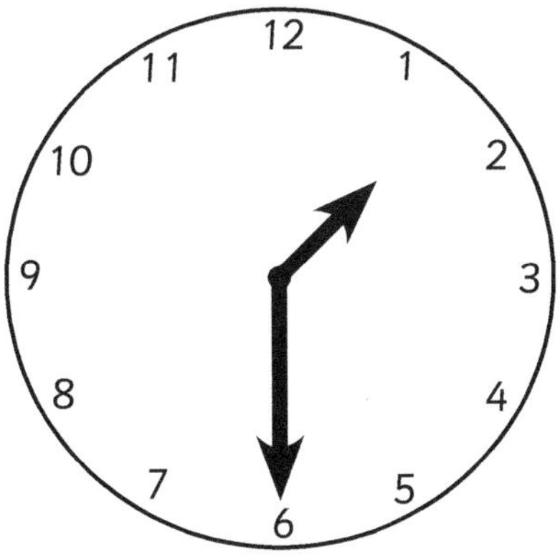

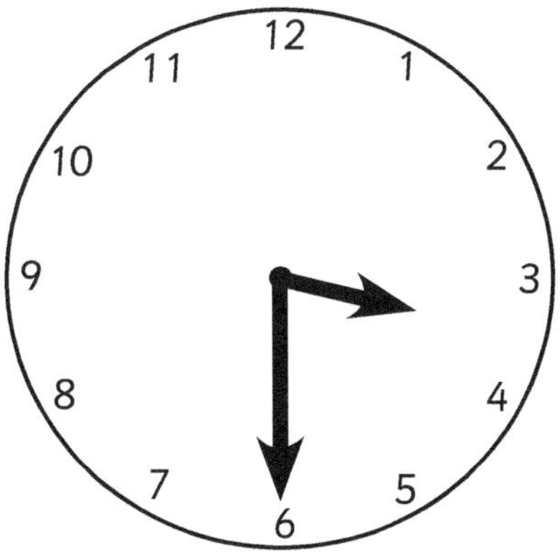

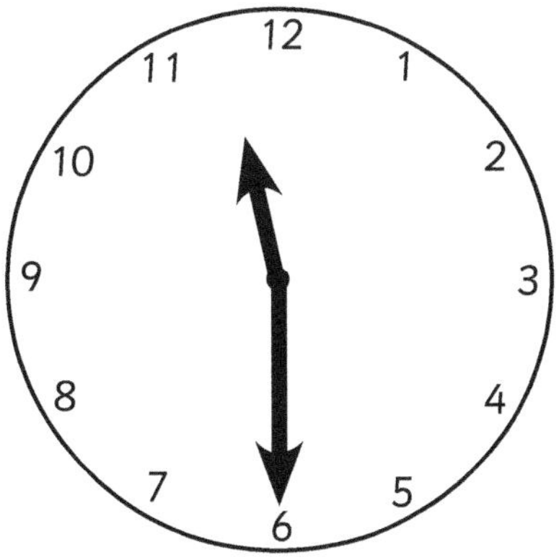

More doubles

7 + 7 = **14**   Double 7 = **14**

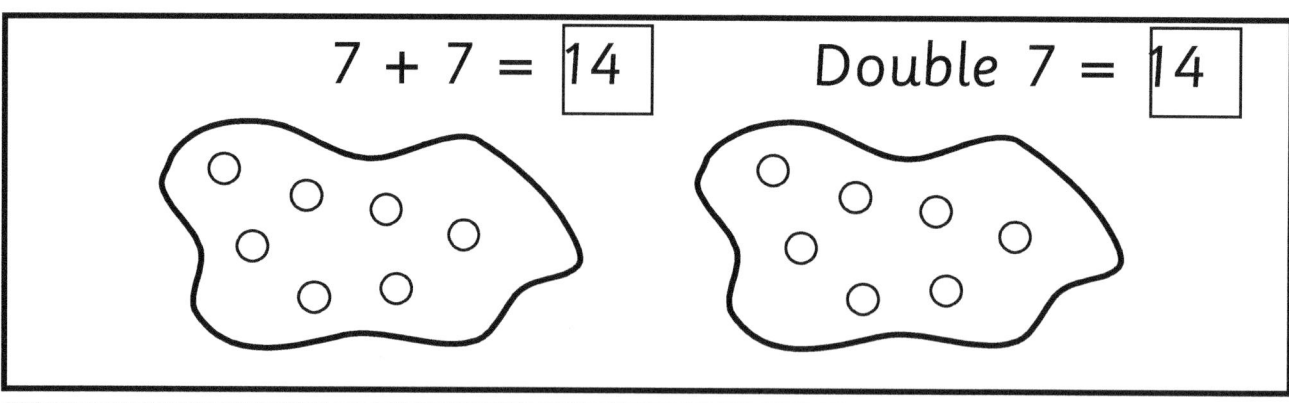

8 + 8 = ☐   Double 8 = ☐

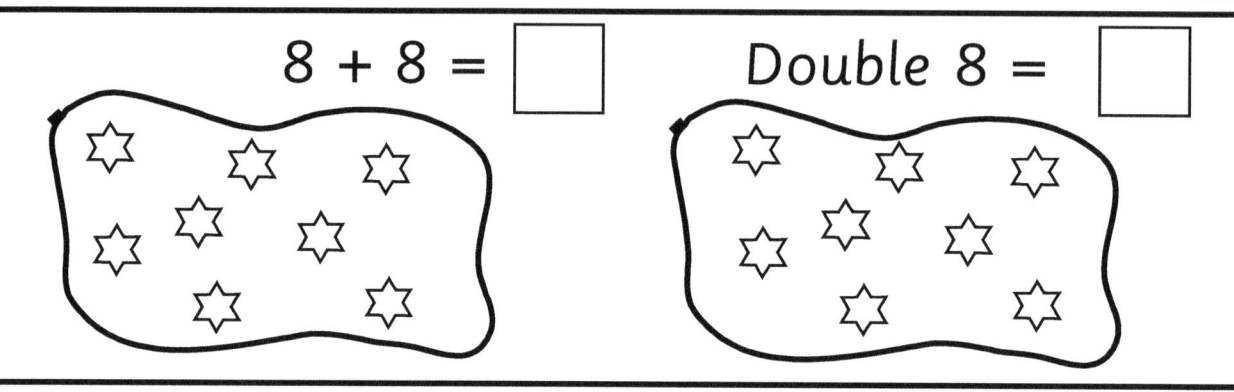

9 + 9 = ☐   Double 9 = ☐

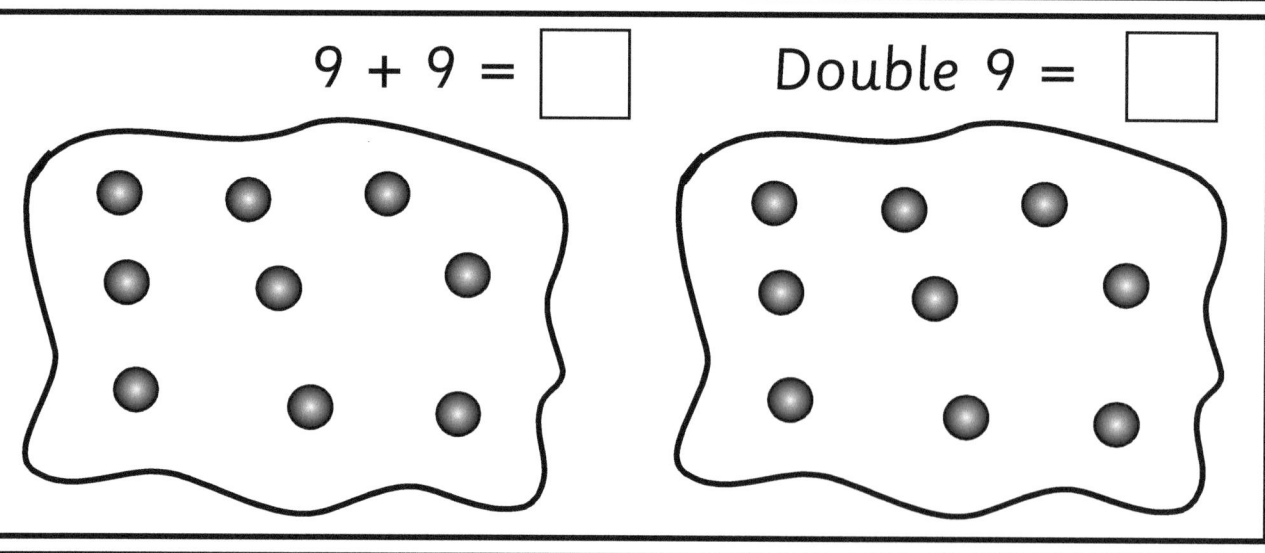

10 + 10 = ☐   Double 10 = ☐

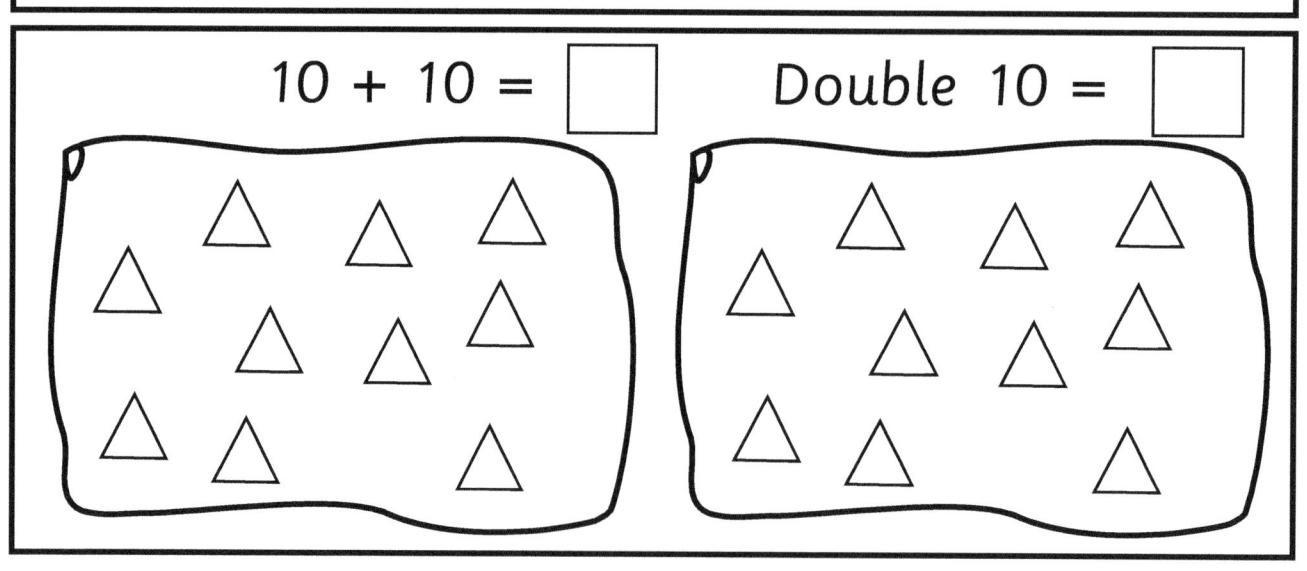

Adding to 10

 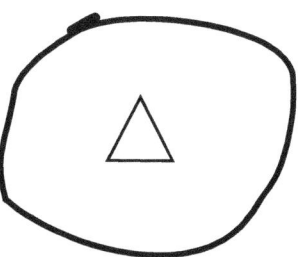 10 + 1 = ☐

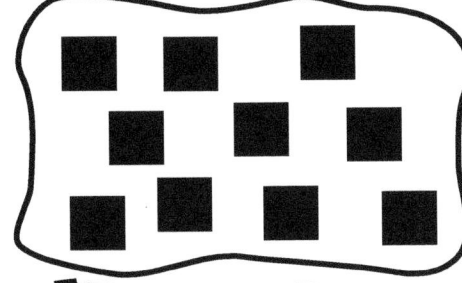 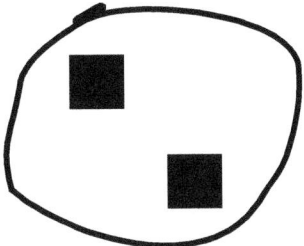 10 + 2 = ☐

 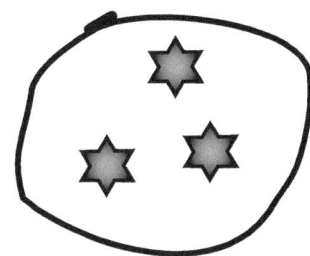 10 + 3 = ☐

  10 + 4 = ☐

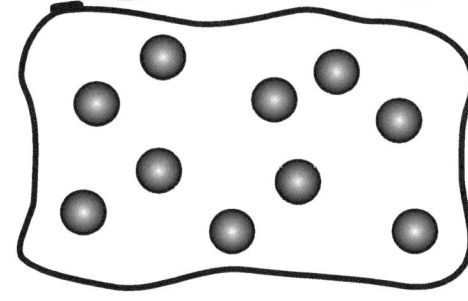 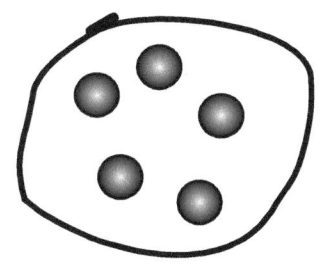 10 + 5 = ☐

Match the questions and answers.

10 + 1	twelve
10 + 2	fourteen
10 + 3	eleven
10 + 4	fifteen
10 + 5	thirteen

27

Adding to 10

  $10 + 6 =$ ☐

 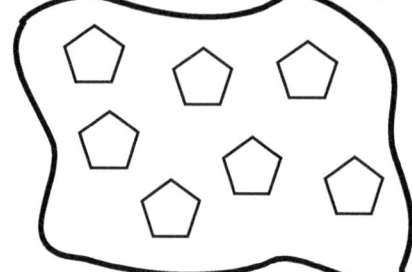 $10 + 7 =$ ☐

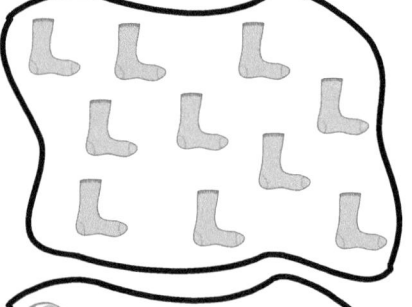 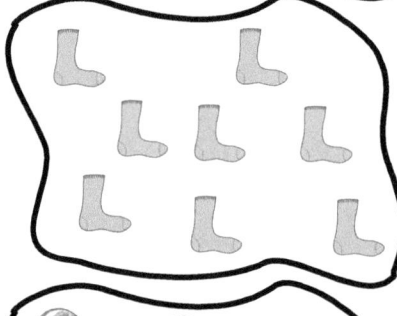 $10 + 8 =$ ☐

  $10 + 9 =$ ☐

  $10 + 10 =$ ☐

10 + 6	twenty
10 + 7	eighteen
10 + 8	sixteen
10 + 9	seventeen
10 + 10	nineteen

Money

Write the value for each coin.

1p   2p   5p   10p   20p   50p

How much is here?

Problems

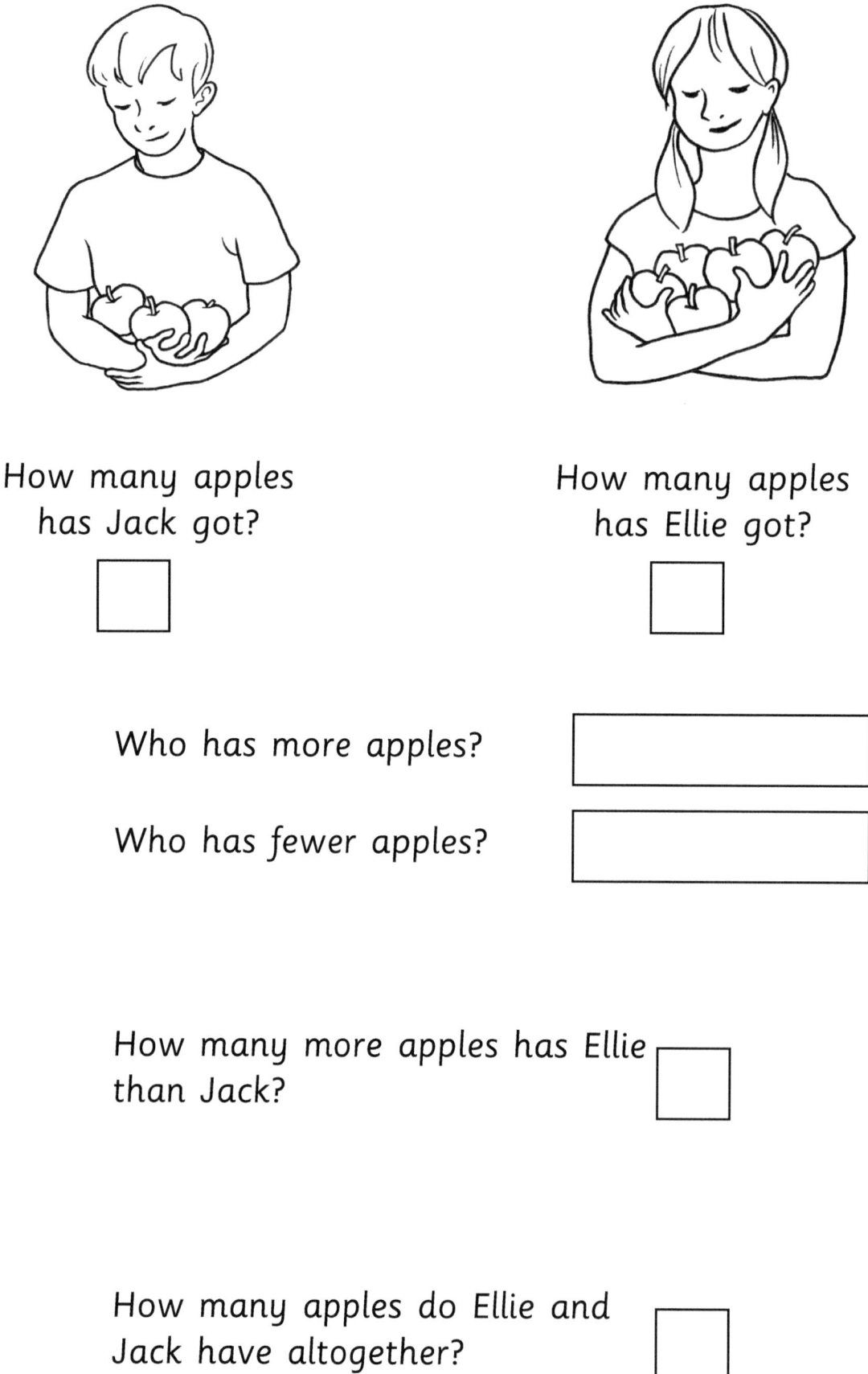

How many apples
has Jack got?

How many apples
has Ellie got?

Who has more apples?

Who has fewer apples?

How many more apples has Ellie
than Jack?

How many apples do Ellie and
Jack have altogether?

Shape

Match these shapes to their names.

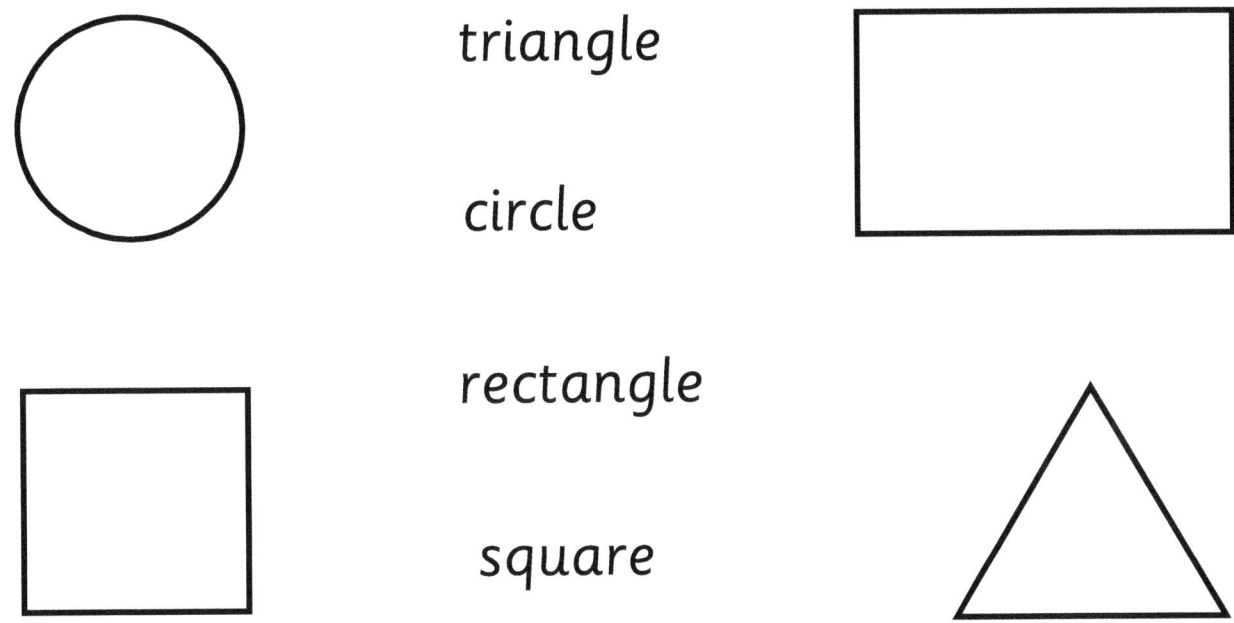

triangle

circle

rectangle

square

Write the words.

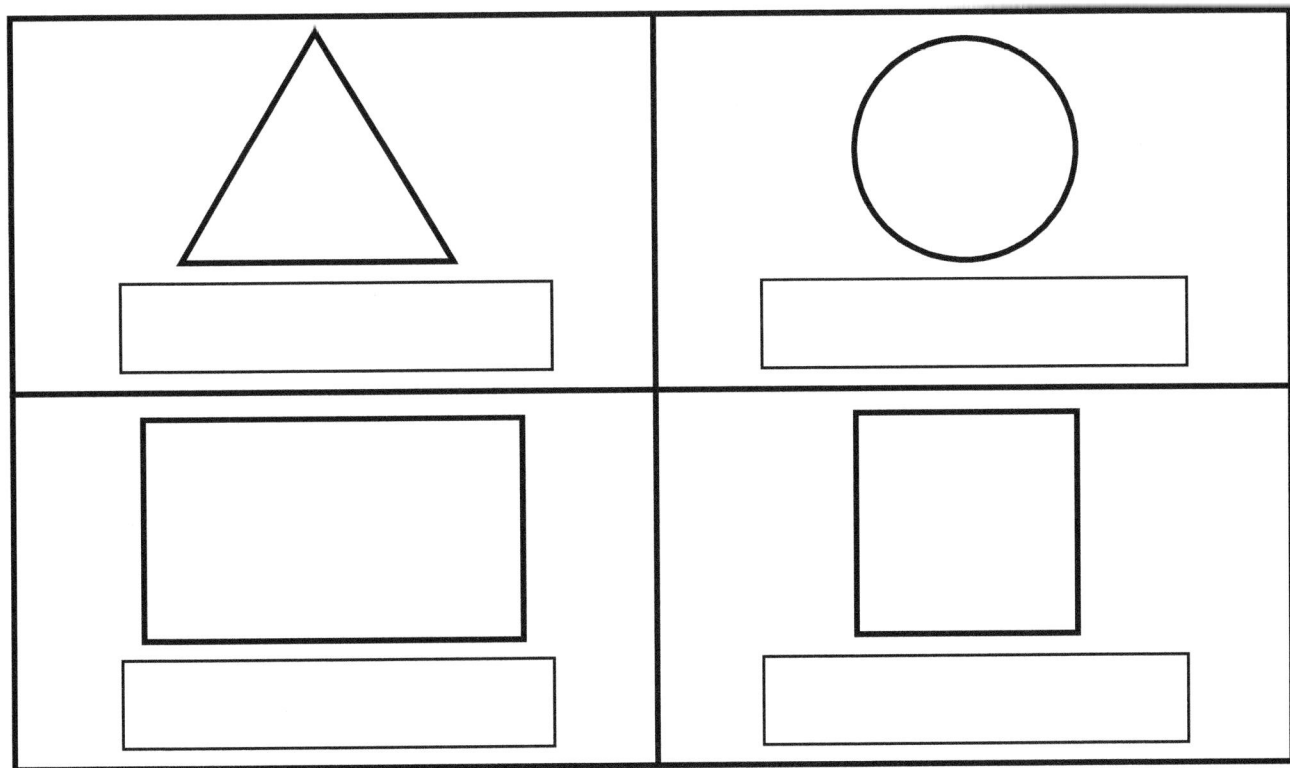

Mixed problems

4 + 3 = ☐   8 − 2 = ☐

Double 6 = ☐   Double 10 = ☐

Half of 12 = ☐   Half of 2 = ☐

5 − 5 = ☐   6 + 5 = ☐

Today is ....

Tomorrow will be ....

Yesterday was ....

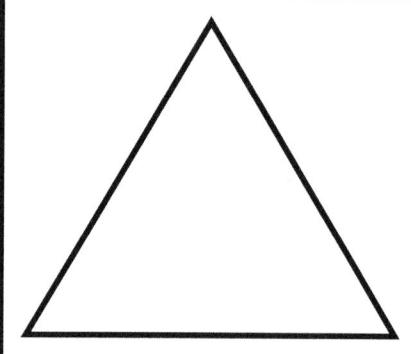

Colour half of this triangle.

The clock shows

....

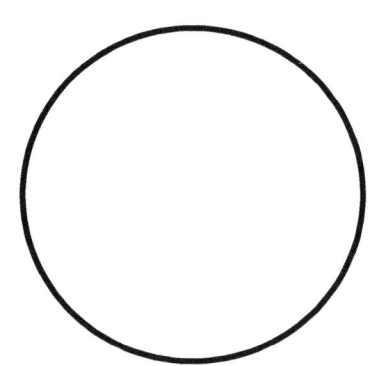

This is a

....